Julio Popper

The Popper Expedition, Tierra del Fuego

A Lecture Delivered at the Argentine Geographical Institute, 5th March

1887

Julio Popper

The Popper Expedition, Tierra del Fuego
A Lecture Delivered at the Argentine Geographical Institute, 5th March 1887

ISBN/EAN: 9783337020477

Printed in Europe, USA, Canada, Australia, Japan

Cover: Foto ©Andreas Hilbeck / pixelio.de

More available books at **www.hansebooks.com**

EXPLORATION OF TIERRA DEL FUEGO

A LECTURE

DELIVERED AT THE ARGENTINE GEOGRAPHICAL INSTITUTE
ON THE 5TH OF MARCH, 1887,

BY

JULIUS POPPER, C.E.

At the beginning of last year, during a voyage of exploration which I made to Cape Virgin, I had several opportuni-
ties of observing the opposite coast of the Straits of Magellan.
There, beneath the covering of a dark grey sky, is to be seen
the lofty table-land which, dark and unvarying, forms the
northern extremity of Tierra del Fuego.

A column of blue smoke revealed to us the presence of
man, and at the same time explained the origin of the name
«Tierra del Fuego» (Land of Fire) given to a country whose
average temperature does not exceed six degrees centigrade.

The melancholy aspect of this coast brought to my recollection a curious publication, consisting of a map preserved
in the National Library of Paris, entitled «Tabula geografica
regni Chile». This map, made in the 17th century by the ᴬⁿ map
Jesuit Fathers of that country, shows in the different parts
of Patagonia drawings of Indians, guanacos, and ostriches,
whereas Tierra del Fuego is designed with the figure of an

At 9 p.m., Mr Popper, who was introduced to the audience by Mr Luis A. Huergo, C.E., President of the Institute, commenced his lecture.

In learned and eloquent language, he outlined the principal features of that distant land, and gave a brief resumé of the journey on which he had started on the 7th of the previous September, accompanied by Mr Julius Carlsson (mining engineer), some techinal assistants, and other men—in all, 18 persons.

Mr Popper, at the close of his lecture, declared that a prosperous economic future awaits those regions, for in them the settler can combine the pursuits of gold-mining and sheep-raising.

The lecturer was loudly applauded, and many of those present complimented him on his perilous and brilliant expedition.

In the following pages is given the lecture, with a map of Tierra del Fuego.

(*Bulletin of the Institute*)

LECTURE

AT THE

ARGENTINE GEOGRAPHICAL INSTITUTE

5TH OF MARCH, 1887.

A numerous and select audience assembled by invitation of the council of the Argentine Geographical Institute to hear a lecture by Mr Julius Popper, C.E., on his recent expedition to Tierra del Fuego.

The subject could scarcely be a more attractive one ; and the crowded assembly showed the most marked attention to the interesting data gathered by the intrepid explorer in those vast and hitherto unknown portions of Argentine territory. The lecture-hall was hung round with photographic views representing some of the most striking episodes of the expedition, as well as mountains, rivers, and, other topographical features of the region. In the centre of the hall there was on view a map of Tierra del Fuego, on which the route of the explorer was marked, flanked by trophies of arms and utensils made and used by the Ona Indians. Upon a table were displayed, besides other minerals, specimens of auriferous sands from Páramo, Cape San Sebastian, and the mouth of the Carmen Sylva River ; as well as samples of the bark of the *Drimys Winteri*.

Indian in the act of hurling a javelin. The most remarkable thing in this figure is that the hind part is adorned with a strange prolongation of the backbone, with an inscription attached, «Caudati homines hic» (Here there are men with tails).

Such a vagary of imagination is easily explained in the 17th century, for even at the present day improbable stories are circulated by the civilised men who dwell in close proximity to that region. During my stay at Cape Virgin, I found it impossible to obtain two reports agreeing on every point, though I addressed myself to many who, being attracted by the glitter of gold, dwelt there at that time, amongst them several hunters of seals which sometimes approach the Fuegian coast.

Their reports contained as many contradictions as we find in the published works of Fitzroy, Cook, Darwin, Bove, etc. According to some, Tierra del Fuego was covered with an impenetrable forest inhabited by a race of diminutive and decrepid Indians. According to others, the Indians are men of gigantic stature. Some declared that they had seen no trees, and that the land was sterile and destitute of every sort of vegetation; whereas several others eulogised the fertility of the soil, and «the picturesque beauty of its valleys and mountains». These contradictory reports, which formed a mass of affirmative and negative assertions, led me to the conclusion that Tierra del Fuego must have presented a very great variety of climate, vegetation, and inhabitants according to the region traversed, and that, with the exception of the Oshowia mission, which is cut off from communication on the extreme south of the island by high mountains covered with eternal snow; and setting aside the north-west, where, for some short time past, search has been made for the gold found in the rivers, the greater part of the island

is still a mystery to the civilised world. The vagueness and
uncertainty of the data received naturally increased in my
mind the ardent desire which I already felt of becoming
acquainted with and studying this enigmatical region, situated
in the extreme South of the American continent.

*
* *

On returning to Buenos Aires, I commenced preparations
for an exploring expedition, for which I reckoned on the
valuable cooperation of Dr. Don Joaquín M. Cullen. Having
been duly authorized by the Minister of the Interior on the 6th
of last September, and with the consent of the Minister of
War, to travel accompanied by armed men, I set out on my
voyage to Tierra del Fuego on the 7th of the same month.
I was accompanied by Don Julio Carlsson, engineer of min- Start from Buenos Aires
ing and metallurgy, a few skilled assistants and a body of
chosen laborers, in all eighteen men, determined not to be
daunted by any difficulties that might present themselves.
Though we set sail in a storm, we had a splendid voyage,
which suited our purpose well, as it was important for us to
preserve in good condition the mules and horses, taken on
board at Montevideo.

We reached Punta Arenas in the Straits of Magellan a Punta Arenas
short time before the National festivals of Chili, a circum-
stance which caused a delay of a few days because it was
difficult to find a person disposed to sell horses or to do
any business before the termination of the feasts. On the
other hand, we received during our stay several tokens of
sympathy from the Governor and people of Punta Arenas.

*
* *

We found ourselves in a place whose geographical position, commerce, and industry peculiarly impressed us, being of a character distinct from anything hitherto known.

Situated almost in the centre of the Straits, the colony of Magellan was established forty years ago, and was used as a convict station until 1877, when the convicts and their keepers, having conspired together, revolted and destroyed a great part of the colony. Today it numbers about 1800 inhabitants, belonging to all nationalities. It forms a central station of outlet and supply for the grazing farms established a short time ago along the northern coast of the straits, and it is of similar service to the vessels which annually sail towards the southern coast of Tierra del Fuego in search of seals. Of late years, the shipwreck of the steamer «Arctic» and the discovery of gold at Cape Virgin have contributed powerfully to the development of this colony, and the inhabitants boast of not having left either on the skeleton of the vessel or in the sands of the Cape anything worth mentioning. From a social point of view, the place is not devoid of interest. I have visited many communities of varied character and formation, but I declare that I have seen nothing similar to this colony, which exists because its geographical situation requires it, which takes no account of the future—believing, no doubt, that it is assured—, which opens its doors at 11 in the morning, and whose greatest concern is to know where the dance, picnic, or banquet will take place the next day. Even the laborer from the mines, who returns after six months of tedious toil, spends his little all in amusements, going down the scale of intoxicating liquors, beginning with champagne, and concluding a few days afterwards with frequent libations of caña. While speaking of these people, it is a pleasure to call to mind the agreeable hours which the traveller enjoys in the company of some distinguished families who have succeeded in introducing into this distant region European customs and comforts.

The festivities being over, we were at last enabled to purchase pack-horses. In a few hours we were in Tierra del Fuego, camping out at Bahía del Porvenir (Future Bay).

*
* *

The name of this bay is derived from the hopes aroused by discovering that the rivers between this point and Bahía Inútil (Useless Bay) bring down gold in their course to the sea. It was then, and it is still, believed, that a great future is in store for this place. Gold is the great attraction. The smallest particle of the precious metal found on the surface of the earth agitates the minds of the people more than thousands of acres of good grazing lands, fertile meads and luxuriant forests. What matters that it requires hourso labor to find a second particle of gold dust? We must have some fixed object in view in this age of steam, electricity and powerful machinery. Do we not hear of enormous quantities of gold extracted from the bowels of the earth even in places where individual labor gives no result whatever; and when the rumour spreads does it not give rise to all sorts of exaggerations? The gold-hunting epidemic breaks out and before long claims its victims from all classes and all ranks of society.

From Porvenir Bay to the River Santa-María is a distance of about three leagues. After crossing the picturesque valley «de los Estrechos», the land begins to rise rapidly; and crossing some slopes, covered for the most part with small brushwood, (*empetrum rhubrum*), we come on marshy flats, alternating with good pasture land, until we find ourselves face to face with an enormous ravine running in a south-westerly direction, at

Porvenir Bay

The Santa María river.

the bottom of which the yellow waters of the Santa Maria noisily follow their zig-zag course.

The lofty cliffs hollowed out in the course of ages by the pent-up waters rendered our descent difficult. At every mo‧ment the ground broke away beneath the weight of our bod‧ies, and we were often obliged to hold on with our hands at a height of thirty or forty feet above the level of the river. Following the course of the water, at a distance of a few metres I suddenly found myself close to a *placer* (a place where gold is washed out on the spot where found). Eight men were engaged shovelling sand into a channel called a «sluice», through which a strong current of water from the river passes. My acrobatic efforts to descend the preci‧pice did not for one moment call off the attention of these men, so absorbed were they; and when they did deign to notice me their looks were anything but flattering. When the mayordomo was informed that my object was to take a photogrophic view of the *placer* be became more affable, and I learned that it belonged to a Greek named Cosme Spiro; and that by uninterrupted work they extracted 30 or 40 grammes of gold daily, which was considered a very satisfactory result in that region.

Descending a couple of miles farther, and still keeping along the course of the river, I found another placer being worked by an Englishman. I was informed that the claim had been acquired by an Argentine company. The system of working is identical with that used in all places where a natural current of water is available. I shall just give an outline of that system. Certain rectangular boxes, from 30 to 40 centimetres wide and 4 metres in length, are telescoped along a declivity of 5 per 100, with a current of water so graduated as to permit the descent of the particles of gold, which, by their specific gravity, fall to the bottom

A placer

Method of working.

and remain there, whilst the sand, being lighter, is carried on to the lower part of the apparatus. The large North American machines, of which mention has lately been made in this city, are simply hydraulic works made to carry the water where it is most needed, making use at the same time of the hydrostatic pressure to disintegrate and wash the sands. The large establishments known in North America as *Hydraulic Minings* bring to my recollection the gold mining works carried on in the Iberian peninsula no less than twenty centuries ago, of which a remarkable description has been handed down to us by Pliny.

On our way from Santa María to Bahía Inutil we met with a series of almost insurmountable obstacles, so that we had to labor incessantly for five days to cross a space which is scarcely two leagues in breadth. On ascending the heights of Sierra Balmaceda the snow began to obstruct our passage seriously, and we were obliged to ply our shovels almost constantly, braced to the work by a temperature the maximum of which did not exceed three degrees. The splendid panorama before us and of which these heights commanded a view, fully recompensed us for our labor. Towards the west, At the summit of the Cordillera spread out like a geographical map, appeared Cape Monmouth, with its snowy *lagunas* of phantastic shape; the Straits of Magellan, whose foggy atmosphere scarcely allowed a glimpse of the Continental coast; to the southwest Dawson Island, with its dense evergreen forests. Towards the south the white mountain range overlooking Beagle Canal, and far away, standing out on the horizon, Mount Darwin and Mount Sarmiento, which, like gigantic sentinels of those Antarctic lands, raise their heads covered with eternal snow far above the region of tempests..........

*
* *

Next day, on descending the southern slope of the Sierra, a new difficulty presented itself. We came upon a space densely covered with bushes of the genus *calceolaria* and dense groves consisting for the most part of the *berberidae*, the *empetrum rhrubrum* and *myrtus mummularia*, which seriously impeded our progress. At every step the vegetation became more and more luxuriant, increasing in height and density, until we were obliged to come to a standstill. Before us was the forest, a solid wall, without outlet or opening, surrounding us on all sides so that at certain times we could neither advance nor go back. It was a gloomy thicket. The ground was covered with uprooted tree trunks and masses of humid and decomposed vegetable matter.

We noticed particularly immense beech trees (*fagus betuloides* and *antarctica*), and in similar abundance the *drimys winteri*, a species of magnolia. Several of these trees were also in a state of decomposition and liable to fall at a touch, and it afforded us no little amusement to pull up and lift trunks of trees of two feet in diameter with less effort than is necessary to raise objects of trifling weight. I have brought specimens of the bark of the magnolia of which I have spoken, and I find it very like that of the cinnamon tree in appearance and aromatic properties. I am informed that the bark is used as a specific for the cure of scab in sheep on some of the farms in Magellan; and as the tree is known to grow in the woods in the Argentine portion of the territory, I believe the day is not far distant when the sheep-farmers will use this native article instead of imported specifics, and that it will prove at the same time efficacious and economical.

For two days we struggled against the almost insurmontable difficulties of the forest, being obliged frequently to make use of our hatchets to open a way; but at times we had the chagrin to see all our efforts frustrated and our perse-

Thickets

Antarctic forest

A new cure for sheep-scab

verance unrewarded, for it not unfrequently happened that
we came upon the brink of a deep hollow or precipice, and,
after hours of tedious labor, were obliged to retrace our steps
and seek out another passage. By constantly consulting the
compass we at last succeeded in gaining the shore in latitude
53° 25'; and longitude 70° 9' W. of Greenwich.

*
* *

Once released from the mournful silence of these woods,
we advanced towards the east by the shore of Useless Bay,
and after crossing some streams we came to the mouth of a
river which seemed to us bewitched. Pyramids of potatoes,
beans, rice, figs and other provisions were piled up in regu-
lar order on the bank.

A surprise

It was in vain that I racked my brain to account for this
strange discovery, until another surprising object appeared
which explained the mystery. A man whose face was fami-
liar to me approached us on horseback at a rapid pace. He
was an old friend from Punta Arenas, who had some months
previously started a placer a few miles from the mouth of the
river. He had only reached there a few days before us, and
had left his provisions on the shore whilst on a visit to the
placer. In his absence the Indians, amazed and puzzled at
finding so many packages the contents of which were, as far
as they knew, useless, placed them on the ground in the
way I have described. They carried off the bags, however;
but the only other injury they did was to mix the salt, sugar
and flour in one heap and to pour on it a quantity of oil.
Mr Wolff, an intelligent and enterprising gentleman, was
the first civilised man to advance thus far. I invited him to
accompany us to the unknown region and he readily and
cheerfully accepted the invitation.

One day later I came to a spot which must soon attract the attention of paleontologists. It is between the meridians 69° 45' and 69° 55' W. of Greenwich, having on the southern side the ccast of Bahía Inútil. The cliff, which here is 80 feet high, presents to view the trunks of petrified trees, some of them transformed into a crystallised calcareous spar.

Fossils

They lie horizontally on the cliff, are from 30 to 40 centimetres in diameter, and show clearly marked concentric circles. Fossil shells also abound, generally embedded in argillaceous rock. As I was obliged to be at the Bay of San Sebastian by a certain date, it was quite impossible for me to devote sufficient time to the study of this interesting spot; but I intend to do so in another excursion.

* *
*

From trigonometrical observations taken I found that this shore is three miles farther north than is indicated in charts. Beyond the meridian 69° 50' the appearance of the surface is notably changed.

The mountains, which up to this point dipped their southern base into the bay, are prolonged to the north-east,

From Bahía Inútil to San Sebastian Bay

and a wide plain slightly undulating and destitute of any vegetation that could even merit the name of a bush, stretches towards the Bay of San Sebastian, being flanked in the distance by two almost parallel mountain ranges. This lead-colored prairie is undermined by the *ctenomys*, a rodent commonly

The ctenomys

called in the Argentine Republic *tucu-tuco*, and in Chile *cururu*. Here the advance of our beasts of burden became very difficult. Sometimes the horses sank to their knees in the burrows and pitfalls. It was useless to seek firm ground; all had been undermined by the *tucu-tuco*.

* *
* *

To the eye, this plain is nothing but a pampa of lugubrious aspect. The few blades of grass that it produces contribute by their yellowish grey color to imprint on the place the stamp of extraordinary melancholy. Not a single guanaco, or even a fox, to enliven the scenery. The repulsive owl alone is to be seen. Appearance of the plain. It casts an angry look at us as we pass at a distance of a single metre and then hovers around us in the air, uttering its strident cry, as if to protest against the intrusion of travellers into its ancient abode.

Suddenly, however, there is a change of scene. We enter one of those glades (*cañadas*) which can only be seen when The glades. one approaches within two or three hundred yards.

The herbage becomes green, and the crystalline waters of the river which flows through the glade are peopled by numerous aquatic birds; ducks, flamingos and bandurrias. Close by a fox glides through the tall grass and stops a short way off to stare at us with curiosity; farther on a guanaco tries to reach the nearest height to salute us with its well-know neigh-like cry, which at times resembles the laugh of a human being.

*
* *

It was in one of these glades that we first met the natives of Tierra del Fuego. I had parted from the expedition and advanced some distance, acompanied by two others, when we suddenly came in sight of a body of twenty-five or thirty Indians, followed by some dogs. Our first impulse was to place ourselves on the defensive and to prepare our Win- Body of Indians. chester rifles, and we observed that the Indians did the same with their bows and arrows; but we remained for some time motionless observing each other. I then thought it well to raise a handkerchief as a token of friendship, but it produced

a very strange effect, for the Indians, as if panic-stricken, took
to flight and crossed the river. One only remained behind,
who tried to carry what seemed to be a heavy bundle, and
whom we soon overtook. She was a female of about 38 years
of age, of tall stature, and covered with a cloak of guanaco
skin. With her face painted with red ochre and her mouth
white with foam, she was the very personification of terror.
Her features were convulsed, her whole body trembled incessantly, and from time to time she stammered out what seemed to us inarticulate sounds. She pointed toward the south-west,
without doubt, in order to convince us that the bad Indians
were to be found in that direction. It was in vain that we
tried to pacify her, and spoke to her in the Tehuelche and
such other exotic languages as we could master; she could
not understand us. I gave her a biscuit, which she took, no
doubt as a matter of courtesy, for I afterwards learned that
her tribe do not eat such food. A red handkerchief was accepted with much greater pleasure. We took some trouble
to assure her that she was at liberty and that she might go
on her way. Even after she was several hundred yards distant
from us she still turned back and pointed to the south-west.
On examining the bundles which the Indians had left behind,
we found that they contained the carcasses of 500 *tucu-tucos*
rolled up in straw and twigs of bushes, which led me to the
belief that the flesh of this animal must be one of the principal provisions of the Indians.

On the next day we reached the Argentine frontier and
encamped on the shore of one of the small lakes that abound
in those places.

A woman.

* *

We judged the bay of San Sebastian to be very near, and in order to make sure I advanced towards the east, accompanied by four of our men, taking with us the photographic apparatus, with the hope that it would be useful in case of any notable occurrence or accident on the way. At a few hundred yards from us we witnessed a lively scene. Some forty Indians were running in all directions, and on reaching a small hillock we saw an imposing body of men armed with bows and arrows and evidently about to make an attack. This sight was by no means attractive, but though we hesitated a moment, it was necessary to advance, so as to avoid showing fear, which at that moment might cause us much injury; and so, placing my men in line, at a distance of ten metres one from another, we advanced steadily toward the Indians, all the time making friendly signs. I soon became aware that our precautions and insinuating gestures were not disarming the hostile intentions of a crowd of Indians, but rather that we had been gesticulating to some fifty dogs which occupied an abandoned *tolderia* (a collection of Indian dwelling)—huts of the most primitive and wretched construction that it is posible to imagine. It was in fact a work very inferior to that performed by certain brute animals. The encampment consisted of fourteen circular hollow spaces excavated to a depth of twenty or twenty-five centimetres, each being about a metre and a half in diameter. Arches, made of the branches of the *Libocedrus Tetragonus*, placed to the west of each hollow, some bundles of dry grass, which in some instances covered them, and fragments of skin, formed the entire archi- tecture of these huts, which at a distance presented such an alarming appearance.

An Indian encampment

A large number of dogs of all sizes, of a species very like the « canis dingo » of Australia, were scampering in all directions, terrified by our appearance, and forming a most infer-

nal concert with their pitiful howling. The ground was covered with the bones of guanacos, sea shells, the skins of
tucu-tucos and the remains of birds; and in the midst of the
spoils we saw a human being, who shook her arms and bab-
bled guttural sounds. She was an old woman, not less than
75 years of age, in a state of most repugnant nakedness,
and of terrible aspect. Propitiating her as far as we were
able, thanks to a red handkerchief and an empty match-box
which I presented, I tried to converse with her; but it was
useless; nor could I succeed in taking a photograph of that
queer specimen of humanity. Whenever I prepared the apparatus and covered my head with the black cloth to get a
focus, she imagined her life was in danger and gave signs
of indescribable terror. She gesticulated frightfully, tossed
herself about with the wildest contortions, leaped and scream-
ed and finally threw herself at the foot of the tripod, with
the manifest, though vain, intention of destroying the apparatus. Though I tried every means, I was unable to pacify her,
and despairing of coming to an understanding with this race
of men, I returned, acompanied by the canine concert, which
had not ceased for one moment.

On the following day we came in sight of the Bay of San
Sebastian; in lat. 53° 15' and long 68° 13'. Standing on a bluff
which showed every sign of having been formerly washed
by the sea, we were separated from the shore of the bay by
a piece of grassy land covered with water, about a league in
extent. As it was the beginning of October I conjectured
that the large quantity of water was produced by the thaw-
ing of the snows on the mountains to the right of us. Ex-
pecting to find dry soil by continuing towards the slope of
the hills, we advanced towards the south; but after wading
for an hour through the flooded land, sometimes with the
water reaching to our waists, and feeling the ground shaking

under our feet, we came upon a deep current in the middle of the flooded plain, which obliged us to go back. We then faced north-wards, where we found a passage, and returned The San Martin River along a wide beach of dry clay in search of an encampment at the mouth of the River San Martin—a name given it by us, inasmuch as it winds its tortuous course for a great length along the meridian which indicates the line of demarcation between the Argentine Republic and Chili. From that day our journey presented a series of accidents and events of the greatest interest. Sometimes these were so serious that they threatened both our lives and the success of the expedition. I shall publish the details when the series of explorations; undertaken to that region is finished, and which I commenced more than a year ago. For the present I shall content myself with giving in a general way a rapid description of that distant country whose mysterious interior I had the good fortune to be the first to explore.

*
* *

Situated on the extreme south of the American continent, torn from the mainland by the powerfull action of two ocean Topogra-phical as-pect currents, and intersected by innumerable canals, straits, gulfs, bays, and inlets, Tierra del Fuego presents a picture so full of orographical and climatological contrast that it is impos- Orography sible to treat of it without first tracing its physical and natural limits. To give a bird's-eye view, then: the island presents on the extreme south-west a montain range whose summits, covered with perpetual snow, reach the height of 7000 feet above the level of the sea. From this range, which is the nucleus of the orographic system of the island, two great rectangular chains branch off, one extending to the south, and the other to the west of Tierra del Fuego. From these, which are intersected by Useless Bay, two secondary ridges are again detached, which follow a parallel course towards the north east of the territory. The first of these chains marked in my map *Carmen Sylva*, a name which I gave it in honor of the Queen of Romania, crosses the middle of the land, sloping down to the lofty cliffs which face the Atlantic and which form the bold promontory of Cape San Sebastian. The second, rapidly rising at Cape Boqueron, abruptly stretches out its diagonal articulations towards the Straits of Magellan, and then sinks gradually so as to merge into the lofty table-land inclosed between Cape Espiritu Santo and the Bay of San Sebastian.

Plains many square miles in extent, for the most part irregularly undulating and covered with innumerable lochs, marshes and stagnant pools, with here and there a streamlet of cristalline water whose course, marked by an emerald-green stripe, contrasts agreeably with the sombre hue of the surrounding country; while the south and west, with their towering mountains, immense glaciers, noisy cascades, and dense forests, complete the varied topographical picture of Tierra del Fuego.

From a physical point of view, this territory may be divided into two great regions, differing entirely in nature, climate, Physical division geological formation, and vegetation. The first division includes the south-west of the island, with its snowy mountains, its woods, and canals. Here dwell the *Jaghan* and *Alicaluf* Indians, a low-sized, almost decrepid, race. The second is the north eastern region, destitute, for the most part, of trees, where broad pampas take the place of woodlands, and where the inhabitants are exclusively *Onas*, a race of robust Índians—agile men, of imposing stature. The greater part of Argentine Tierra del Fuego is included in this region, and to its thorough exploration I devoted my last journey, on which I now have the honour to speak. Omitting my travels in Chilian territory, the result of which I shall publish when I have realized the third expedition which I have in contemplation, and taking Cape Espiritu Santo as a starting point, I met, from the extreme north of the Argentine territory to Cape Peñas, seven rivers, whose names, geographical situation, distances, and direction, I took the liberty of inscribing with indelible paint on a large erratic rock which stands on the broad beach of Cape San Sebastian, my only object in so doing being to facilitate the exploration of these rivers by the travellers who may come after me. The following are the names written on the rock: Hydrography

River *Juarez Celman*, direction south, distance 30 miles; flows into the sea in lat, 53° 46'.

River *Carmen Sylva*, south, distance 23 miles; flows into the sea in lat. 53° 40'.

Rivulet *Gama*, west, 5 miles.

River *San Martin*, distance 11 miles, west; flows into the bay in lat. 53° 16'.

River *Cullen*, north; flows into the sea in lat. 52° 53'.

Rivulets *Alpha* and *Beta*, north; flow into the sea in lat. 52° 44° and 45' respectively.

The largest of these rivers, to which we have given the name of Juarez Celman .in honour of the new President of the Republic, who took office almost at the very date on which we arrived at that important body of water, rises in the eternal snows of the mountain range, and winds its way across the central part of the island. During the time that I observed this river — in the beginning of the month of November — its velocity was 1 metre 10 centimetres per second, and the smallest width I found at low tide, for a distance of 28 kilometres from the mouth, was 70 metres, whereas at high tide it measured 800 metres across. The water of this River Juarez Celman river is transparent, with a surface temperature of 8 degrees centigrade.

As I did not expect to find so important a river on the island, I was not provided with the necessary means to determine how far it was navigable. I believe, however, judging from what I have seen and examined, that at some future time this river will surely contribute largely to the industrial development of those regions.

*
* *

The climate of Tierra del Fuego presents a vast field for observation. In order to give an idea of the meteorology of the island, I shall take the liberty of reproducing a leaf from my diary of travels, dated the 21st of last November:

Meteorology

«Encamped on the River Cullen. Lat. 52° 52' S., long. 68 25' W. Time 5.30 a.m. Barometer 747ᵐ. (rising). Thermometer + 7° centigrade. Maximum for the day before 14°, minimun 1° above zero. A cloudy sky, blasts of wind from the west; nothing new during the night; but some native dogs which prowl around our camp attract the attention of the guards.

A leaf from my diary

8 a.m.—Barometer 747ᵐ. North-west wind, 15 metres per second. Thermometer 10°. We are engaged in loading our beasts of burden. I remark that they have grown exceedingly fat this last month. Castro and Grassano chase a guanaco, which escapes after a short run by rushing into the sea. It is useless to expect it to return. To-morrow, perhaps, it will be found cast ashore some miles farther to the south. The river has risen enormously. The tides are at their highest, for the summer solstice is approaching.

Bill of fare for breakfast:

M E N U

Wild celery soup with English sauce.
Kaiken eggs with seal oil.
Chloephaga Magellanica with Worcestershire sauce.
Guanaco steak with *Fuegian* celery.
Coffee without sugar.

(I may remark that at this time our provisions were nearly reduced to three bottles of English sauce and two pounds of coffee.)

10 a.m.—Barometer 748^m. Thermometer + 9°. Rain from north-west. We are ready to march. The castor oil has worked miracles. Matthew and Leopold have recovered; Manuel alone is still suffering from cholic, if he is not inventing an excuse to obtain another glass of the anti-cholera liquor. The brackish water which we were obliged to drink at the bay of San Sebastian has produced the epidemic. We test the sand extracted yesterday from the bed of the river. It leaves a residue of magnetite and some diminutive garnets. We issued forth towards the north-east. Azimuth 327°.

11 a.m.—The barometer is rising. Thermometer + 6° Heavy snow from the south-west. We find ourselves on an elevated plain covered with grass suited for sheep. Not a single bush to be seen on the horizon.

11.30 a.m.—Barometer 748.5^m. Thermometer + 5°. The wind blows at the rate of 10 metres per second with heavy hail. The Montevidian horses and mules are indignant at the weather of Tierra del Fuego. They shake their heads violently, and keep the left ear twitching to get rid of the hail that enters its funnel-like concavity.

2 p.m.—Barometer 750^m. Thermometer + 10°. The wind blows 25 metres per second, with a cloudy sky, 5/10.

For the last two hours we have had rain, snow, hail and wind alternately, but at certain times we have enjoyed all together. Two hours ago we left our horses. We are on the bank of the rivulet *Beta*. We remark a fire made by Indians, towards the west, at a distance of about two leagues. The valley crossed by the stream produces some bushes of the *Berberis axifolia*, and offers excellent pasture. We are surprised at the abundance of game. Here is a covey of the *Chloephaga Magellanica*, with its young, searching for worms in the grass; there a pair of ducks, *Anas cristata*, gliding over the limpid surface of the stream, and followed by a new generation of their own species. On all sides there are flocks of birds of different sizes and colors. On descending the valley we remark great animation among its inhabitants. A multitude of ducks and other birds rise with sharp screams and incessant flappings. They fly in circles above our heads, and at times come so near that they almost touch our caps with the tips of their wings.

In the meantime we are busy catching young ones. It is curious to see these tender creatures obeying the instinct of self-preservation, and trying to hide themselves in the burrows of the *tucu-tucos*, behind the bushes or in a tuft of grass. There, with their eyes closed and endeavouring to reduce the size of their bodies to the smallest dimensions, they resignedly await their fate. We secure eighteen, while the *ca ardière* furnishes three geese and eight ducks.

4 p. m.—Barometer 751^m. Thermometer +8°. Sky cloudy, north-west wind.

On advancing out on the strand, something in the shape of an enormous human being attracts our attention. We examine it, and discover that it is a fragment of the conglomerate of the cliff, on which the rain and wind have modelled the outlines of a gigantic statue.

A traveller endowed with a poetic imagination would say that this work of the elements resembles a Colossus seated on the slope of an eminence, in an attitude of meditation, and, absorbed in hope or observation, gazing into the depths of the At· lantic.

We remark on the cliff a dark vein of eight metres in height, which is worthy of attention, and which we intend to study later on. We return to the stream in search of camping ground, and choose the slope of a hill which affords shelter from the wind. Our pack-horses have not yet arrived, so we light three fires to mark the place where their drivers are to stop. We then go to look for guanacos.

7 p. m.—Barometer 753ᵐ. Thermometar +4°. Weather calm. A thick mist comes up slowly from the north. At about four kilometres from the mouth of the stream we saw a guanaco, which we found it easy to catch, favored as we were by the burrows of the *cururus*, which abound here, for whilst the guanaco stumbles into the holes, the dogs, being lighter, easily jump over them. The guanaco is down; the dogs, which now are as ferocious as hyenas, are tearing it to pieces. Our horses can scarcely advance a step over the treacherous ground. Losing all patience, I leave my horse and run the remaining 200 yards in order to give the *coup de grace* to the poor quadruped; but hardly had I reached it when I heard shouts of «Indians! Indians!»

A few hundred yards from the guanaco, not far from the stream, we see several Indians running towards the west, while some native dogs surround a brake. Undoubtedly the bundles of *tuco-tucos* are there, for we know that these dogs stay beside the huts instead of accompanying the inhabitants. Cautiously approaching, we find two Indians sitting among the bushes, who raise their arms in supplication, without doubt in order to show that they are not possessed of bows

or arrows, or, perhaps, to convince us that they belong to the
beautiful sex. Their faces, nevertheless, do not reveal as
much. They are daubed with clay taken from the soil, an
operation probably begun on seeing us approach, for on parts
of the face the clay is still fresh and contrasts with the light
grey colour of the portion that is dry· They are seated on
bundles of straw, which doubtless contain *tucu-tucos* or some
eatables of that sort. They are women of about 30 or 35
years of age, but they scream like new-born babes. Blood is
flowing from self-inflicted wounds on their knees.

We succeed in pacifying one of them, who leaves off
screaming and commences to smile, but our efforts to tran-
quillize the other are useless. She is armed with a sharp
stone, with which she makes incisions in her skin in hori-
zontal lines extending from arm to arm right across the
breast, leaving a white mark which contrasts with the coppery
color of her body. Sometimes drops of blood ooze out
through these marks. It is impossible to calm her, and she
continues making parallel lines with the stone, at the same
time shouting, *Ona, ona! Acá, acá;* the meaning of which I
do not understand. On the other hand, the second female
becomes more amiable; she smiles and shows her small teeth,
of a dark yellowish color near the gums, and offers us some
red ochre in a purse made of the skin of the *Ctenomys.*
We return the compliment and make her a present of two
handkerchiefs. We ask her to stand up, and on doing so we
notice something moving in the bundles of straw. Examining them, we find that they contain three little children
of from four to six years. Their eyes closed, crouching as
if to diminish their size, it seems to us that these little creatures acted on the same impulse as the young of the ducks
we had caught some hours previously, and we find a striking
likeness between the situations of both. Our curiosity

being satisfied, we leave the Indian women and return to the
guanaco, a great part of which has been by this time devoured
by the dogs, which, in the excitement caused by the presence
of the Indians, we had forgotten to drive away.

9 p.m. — Barometer 752.5^m. Thermometer $+ 2^0$. Strong
wind from the south-west, which obliged us to lower our tents
as far as the roof, the edges of which we covered with thick
sods, though even then there was danger of the blasts sweeping
them off into the waves of the Atlantic.» Thus far the
diary.

Although the barometer was rising, we were continually
experiencing variations of weather almost phenomenal. On
the following day the barometer rose another millimetre, with
rain from the north, and I observed that at other times the
barometer had a tendency to fall when the weather is comparatively fine.

Barometer.

This phenomenon has for a long time attracted the attention
of navigators in those regions, and there are few mariners
who in that latitude place much reliance on the readings of the
barometer.

The meteorology of Tierra del Fuego has yet to be studied,
because I do not pretend that the observations of a few months
can establish anything like a fixed rule. Nevertheless, I can
easily account for the atmospheric disturbances in that country.

Atmospheric
disturbances.

There are two causes which make the climate of Tierra
del Fuego the stormiest in the world. One is local, and is
found in the eternal snows and gigantic glaciers that cover
the mountain peaks of the south-west. Thence descends a
continual current of cold air which rushes towards the eastern
coasts and pampas, where, heated by the sun, it becomes an
ascending column, and constantly forms a centre of minimum
barometrical pressure. The other cause, still more powerful, is
found in the maritime currents which flow towards the island;

for, while the south-west is washed by the cold waves of the Atlantic currents, the eastern shores receive the tropical current of Brazil, owing to which the sea water of this zone shows a temperature of 9 degrees. It is, therefore, easy to understand the cause of those blustering winds which, coming from the west, lash that region The west wind begins generally at sunrise. It increases about noon, and in the evenin sometimes acquires a velocity of 40 metres per second. At sunset, when the horizon is tinged with the colors of twilight, the wind almost completely ceases, and is succeeded by a Winter calm of a few hours, during which the traveller may fix his tent, etc. What I have just stated will explain why, in my opinion, it is as easy to abide in those regions in the winter as in the summer, though at first sight such may appear strange.

The reason is to be found in the prolonged periods of calm weather which prevail during this season, while the sun is scarcely six hours above the horizon, and when its oblique rays are incapable of melting the masses of snow spread far over the pampas, whose temperature maintains the equilibrium of the atmosphere. The north winds which generally blow at this time, and the Brazilian current referred to, contribute Thermometer by their warmth to modify the temperature, so that the minimum seldom reaches 10 degrees below zero. The maximum which I observed during the expedition was + 23° and the minimum — 6°; the average temperature from 6 a.m. to 6 p.m. was + 11.5°, and the average for the night + 2°. I observed that the thermometer generally reaches the maximum about 10.30 a.m. and the minimum at 10 at night. With regard to the barometer, I have not been able to come to any conclusion, though I have taken observations three or four times a day. Not unfrequently a fall in the mercury preceded dry weather and west wind.

At other times it rose and fell rapidly in the same state of the weather. These phenomena, which have formed the subject of much fruitless discussion, are, in my opinion, caused by the circumstances I have just brought to your notice, as well as by the peculiar configuration of the land; for whilst a storm is raging high up in the mountains, in the pampas calm weather may prevail. I am convinced that the only way to arrive at an exact conclusion would be to mark the state of the weather simultaneously at Oshowia, Punta Arenas, Cape Virgin, and some spot on the Pacific, and to compare notes afterwards on the observations of a number of years.

In this way a result would be obtained which might enable the navigator to trust to the barometer in that region. We could not, of course, in an expedition so limited in time as ours was, expect to take pluviometrical observations of any permanent value. I may mention, however, that during our journey we had twenty-one days of rain; two in the month of September, three in October, ten in November, and six in December.

To conclude the meteorological picture of the island, I feel bound to mention a phenomenon which will undoubtedly interest the writers of romance. From the river San Martin as far as the extreme north of the Bay a clayey plain more Fata Morgana than three miles wide stretches for a distance of four miles. The most curious thing about this strand is that it is entirely dry, presenting in its complete flatness the aspect of an immense square covered with asphalt.

On crossing it for the first time, a wonderful sight surprised me. It seemed to me that I was in the centre of a circular plain whose circumference was washed by the placid waters of the ocean. I went on, following the line of 5°, marked by the magnetic needle, and when I had advanced some miles I fancied myself still in the centre of the plain. Tired of walking without having apparently made any progress, I stopped to await the arrival of the horses that I expected to come that way, when, suddenly, I perceived a group of gigantic beings rapidly approaching me. I smiled on discovering that it was only the reflection of the horses and their riders made on the surface of the mud, and that what I supposed to be the ocean was simply the image of the sky, reproduced by the same refraction.

It was a magnificent optical delusion which fascinated us. I had observed a similar spectacle in the immediate neighborhood of Port Said, in Egypt; but the brilliant colours of the picture in Tierra del Fuego were wanting in that. A guanaco running along the plain was like two palm trees whirled along by the wind. A number of dogs belonging to the Indians took, when running, the form of huge frogs which jumped into the waters of that imaginary ocean. On turning to look at the horses I thought I saw something like an immense wood of majestic oaks, bending before the wind to an angle of 45 degrees.

This phenomenon can be seen daily on the shore of the bay, and the explanation thereof is indeed very simple. It is found in the temperature of the atmosphere, the strata of which, being of different densities, possess different properties of refraction. The clay warmed by the sun, and the atmosphere cooled by the west wind, produce these deceitful appearances, similar to the *fata morgana* on the coast o Sicily, to which the French give the name of *mirage*.

* * *

Geology   The geological study of the Island reveals the fact that the land is rapidly rising. Extensive tracts, today covered

with grass, formed at a comparatively recent period the
bottoms of broad bays and wide canals, covered by the briny Upheavals
waves of the ocean.

The cliffs which commence a few miles to the north of
Cape Sunday, and which continue far inland; those which
border on Cullen Valley, five miles from the sea; and those
at the south of the Bay of San Sebastian, now divided by a
level tract a kilometre wide, are convincing evidence of this
subterranean disturbance. But what especially satisfied me
as to the rapid action of geocentric forces was the result of
the trigonometrical measurements which I took between Capes
Sunday and Peñas. I verified the fact of the coast-line being
three kilometres farther out than it was when Fitzroy visited
it fifty years ago. A similar phenomenon of still more recent
date is seen on the western shores of the Bay of San Sebastian. I have mentioned some particulars in reference to
this when treating of the meteorology. The waves of the
ocean have also retired from this place, but the land has not
yet had sufficient time to accumulate vegetable soil, and the
clay appears just as it must have been when it was covered
by the waters, the only difference being that the contraction
produced by drying has formed a network of rifts and clefts,
which by their symmetrical designs make the surface appear
as if artificially ornamented.

Another proof which also reveals the pre-existence of a
maritime canal that joined the Bay of San Sebastian to Use- Ancient chan-
nel
less Bay, consists in the erratic rocks which I met with in
crossing this region. Some of these blocks measure fully
eight cubic metres.

They are for the most part granite, gneiss, and cyenite,
through which a vein of white or yellow quartz sometimes Erratic rocks
runs. I found them quite isolated in the midst of the
plain; not a fragment of the same kind of stone being found

even at a great distance. Judging from their appearance, they must have been transported from afar by icebergs; the latter melting, the rocks were precipitated to the bottom, assuming on their passage through the water the vertical position in which they rest. On seeing them, one is forcibly reminded of the famous tower of Pisa, which, a marvel of equilibrium, threatens to fall at every moment.

I have given the name of *The Three Sphynxes* to a place situated in lat. 53° 15′ and long. 68° 47′, where three of these rocks, 300 metres apart, spoke to me, notwithstanding their silence, of geological ages past, when the land which we were now crossing on horseback supported an immense sheet of water, teeming with marine life and bearing on its surface great masses of ice.

Not only in the valleys, but even at a height of 300 metres, I found similar blocks, although in a more decomposed state; their origin is clearly proved by the *Patellae* and *Mytili* shells abundantly scattered in the immediate neighbourhood.

On observing attentively the course of the rivers which empty themselves into the Atlantic, I remarked that all the fluvial arteries have on their south banks a cliff, with the deepest water that the river contains at its base; whereas the opposite bank presents the appearance of wide plains gradually rising towards the north. This observation leads me to conclude that the elevation of Tierra del Fuego has a tendency towards the south-west, which forces the waters of the rivers to excavate beds that are constantly advancing towards the south.

The wide clayey beach on the western coast of the Bay of San Sebastian is simply the work of the river *San Martin*, whose bed, gradually extending, has traversed the entire space from the north to the south of the bay. This same tendency explains why the rivulet *Gama*, which formerly

emptied itself into the south of the bay, terminates at present
in a series of lakes of fresh water which seek the level of
the sea, slowly trickling through the elevated sand of the shore.

Nature's mighty operations often serve to help on the
puny work of man; and it is no doubt in virtue of the
tendency referred to that I have been enabled to obtain
samples from the bed of coal in the range of cliffs to the
south cf Cape Espiritu Santo. This carboniferous bed, which ^{Bed of coal}
near the cape is found at a height of 120 feet, sinks along
with the general dip of the land to a height of six feet,
which enabled us to examine it without much trouble. Whilst
declaring that I have discovered a coal bed on Argentine
territory, I am sorry to be obliged to add that I am not a
candidate for the premium of $ 25,000 offered by the Govern-
ment to the discoverer of this mineral; for the coal which I
found will, perhaps, require to go on improving for about 200
centuries more before it acquires any commercial value. It
is in fact a seam of lignite, exhibiting the trunks and branches
of carbonised trees enclosed in a schist which forms the bulk
of the layer.

But if this discovery is of no commercial value, it is not
devoid of scientific interest, because it proves positively that
this land, stripped to-day of all vegetation, must have presented in times past a physical constitution, climate, and vegetation totally different from what we now behold; and it is
a confirmation of the fact, that the trees of which the bed is
composed belong to a species different from those which are
found in the woods of the south and west.

Herein we present a description of the cliff as it is given
by Engineer Carlsson:

Vegetable earth.............. 0.60 metres
Gravel........................... 1.00   »

Sandy conglomerate.......	9.00 metres
Sandstone......................	3.00 »
Gravel.............................	6.00 »
Carboniferous bed..........	0.70 »
Sandstone.......................	4.00 »
Conglomerates................	22.00 »

Judging from its elevation and general appearance, the explored region must belong to the tertiary formation, being formed of large stratified masses associated with sandstone sometimes laminated, and covered with a layer of from five to twenty feet of coarse gravel or pebbles of a rather angular shape.

Mineralogy The mineral substances which most abound are granitic and felsitic porphyry, diorite, gneiss, granite, serpentine, cienite, trachite. quartz, amphibolite, and petro-silex . I have also met extensive beds of sand of a dark blue color, generally composed of magnetite, and rubies and garnets of a small size.

The only metal I found in a condition fit to be worked was Gold gold—an alluvial gold composed of 90 per cent. of fine gold, 9.5 per cent of silver, and five-thousandths of other substances.

Although Argentine Tierra del Fuego presents traces, or rather indications, of gold in all its extent, the auriferous area which I have discovered shows signs of having recently been formed in lands which a comparatively short time ago were submerged in the depths of the ocean.

*
* *

Argentine Tierra del Fuego is inhabited by an aboriginal Ona Indians race, stout, strong, and muscular, whose stature sometimes exceeds six feet.

Their skin is a light copper color, and of a smooth and greasy feel. Around a large tonsure in the mlddle of the head their dull black hair falls in heavy locks. The oval face is of orthogonal type, the forehead rather narrow, which with the poorly-developed frontal protuberances terminating in prominent and but slightly arched eyebrows, gives to their eyes an expression at once sunken and energetic. Prominent cheek-bones and an almost aquiline nose; a medium-sized mouth, with teeth covered with a yellowish enamel; two or three hairs on the chin, and a pair of hanging and shapeless ears complete a face which reminds one more of the North American Indian than of the *Tehuelches*, who inhabit the other side of the Straits. Their shoulders are square and strong, their chest broad, and, in the men, prominent and rounded, whilst the women generally have flattened bosoms with flacid, hanging breasts, though I have occasionally seen the latter firm and hemispherical.

The women's arms are strong and round; those of the men, sinewy. Their hands are large, with short fingers terminating in flat, square nails.

The Ona Indian is generally of a cumbrous figure; and the size of his abdomen varies extremely, depending as it does on whether he has or has not discussed his Fuegean dinner.

From the abdomen down nature has been less prodigal. The legs, although straight and muscular, are not in proportion to the body, the calves being spare and very poorly developed; the feet are of medium size.

Notwithstanding the severe and stormy climate of that land, the inhabitants wear no clothing save a guanaco-skin cloak, and dwell under the wretched shelter afforded by a couple of branches stuck in the ground to windward, their only roof the blue vault of heaven, in which for ever shines the beauteous constellation of the Southern Cross.

The Onas are nomads, as is proved by their tents, which

can easily be removed from one place to another. In winter,
when snow covers the hills and plains, their favorite resorts
are the southern coasts of the Straits of Magellan and the
eastern shores of Tierra del Fuego. The innumerable hollows
or abandoned encampments which I met with in these places,
and around which are to be seen heaps of seashells, clearly
indicate their original object. In spring and summer the men
devote themselves exclusively to hunting the guanaco and the
fox, while the duty of the women is to catch the *tucu-tucos*,
which they do by thrusting a sharp pole from burrow to
burrow ; also to provide fish and shellfish, to prepare skins, etc.

In the beginning of my travels, whenever I met a group of
Indians, I found it difficult to distinguish the sexes, but with
a little practice I have formed an infallible rule : an Indian
carrying a bow is a man; an Indian carrying any heavy
burden is a woman. Besides the bow, the strings of which
they make of the sinews of the guanaco, every Indian is
supplied with a quiver made of sealskin, which contains as many
as 25 arrows tipped with glass or sharp stones. A triangular
piece of skin which they wear on their forehead, and a purse,
or bag, of fox-skin, complete their equipment. I have often
examined the contents of these bags, and I almost always
found, besides eggs, *cururus*, and other food, a piece of iron
pyrite and some other stone, a sort of dry fungus, and a small
purse made of the skin of the *tucu-tuco*, which invariably contained a small quantity of red ochre powder.

The only ornament I observed amongst the matrons of
Tierra del Fuego was a bracelet of perforated calcareous shells,
denoting a self-denial that could not fail to be highly satisfactory to a civilised husband.

Nimbleness, keen sight, etc.   The Onas are extremely nimble. Being obliged to hunt
the guanaco on foot, they run with extraordinary swiftness.
Through curiosity I measured the tracks left in the sand by

an Indian who fled before us, and the length of each stride was 1 metre 90 centimetres.

The wounds which I have seen them inflict on themselves, and which, perhaps, are connected with some superstitious belief, denote strength of mind, and lead me to the conviction that these aborigines can bear, without much suffering, fatigue, cold, hunger, and all kinds of hardship. Their extraordinary endurance when in want of food is specially worthy of admiration, and in connection with this matter I was told a curious incident at the estancia of Mr Stubenrauch, at Gente Grande bay. They had for some time there a native Indian girl of sixteen years of age, who refused to take any kind of food during the first eight days of her captivity.

On the ninth day a sheep was set before her, which, unwillingly and with many grimaces, she at length attacked. The meal lasted three hours; and when, finally, the girl rested from her gastronomic labours, her appearance was such that anyone unaware of the circumstances would have unhesitatingly pronounced her pregnant. Of the sheep all trace, save the bones, had disappeared.

At the same place I learned that this Indian maiden had exceedingly keen sight: she could see a man, a horse, or a sheep at distances quite out of the reach of our vision even with the telescope. I also found out how the Onas make the tonsure I have mentioned. They make use of a whalebone comb, like the large old-fashioned Spanish one, which they pass through the hair on the top of the head, and then apply a red-hot cinder to the hair that protrudes between the teeth of the comb, obtaining by this means the desired object with a neatness and rapidity to be envied by the smartest barber.

With regard to the intellectual faculties of the Onas, they

cannot be much developed, judging by the primitive instru-
ments they make use of in everyday life. These are generally pieces of iron taken from some vessel cast on the shore,
wrapped up and tied to wooden handles with leathern thongs.
To dig the ground, they make use of the shoulder-blade of
the guanaco, and the only vessels they use are large sea
snail shells and marine trumpets. They have no canoes, and
do not devote themselves to fishing. They only gather the
fish stranded at low tide. To catch these they use a species
of harpoon with a bone point. Some intelligent effort is ob-
Weapons, etc. servable in the making of arrows and baskets. The former
are beautifully finished and evenly balanced. With the glass
of bottles picked up on the shore they prepare a special
dart, which they work into form and sharpen by pressing
with the weight of their bodies upon an iron drill. Other
darts are made of hard stone, cut and sharpened in the same
manner.

The baskets are of woven rushes, thick, strong, and, at the
same time, flexible. A cord made of the guanaco's sinew,
placed across the mouth of the basket, does duty as a handle.
To catch birds they use snares made of thin and pliant
whale-bone nooses, which, being hidden in the grass, serve
the same purpose as the well-known wooden-trap for catching
partridges (cimbra), the only difference being that in the
former it is not by an effort of man the trap is closed, but
by the weight of the bird or the animal lured by the
bait.

During the course of the expedition, I tried to enter into
friendly relations with the Indians I met on the way, but, I
Farm at Gente am sorry to say, without any success. Instead of recirrocat-
Grande
ing our kind feelings, they invariably showed a marked tendency to make war on us. I believe I can trace the origin
of this persistency to the following fact: Some few years ago

the British Consul at Punta Arenas, Mr Stubenrauch, on seeing the beautiful plains at Gente Grande Bay, resolved to establish a sheep farm there, and had some houses built; he enclosed large spaces with wire fences, and carried over some sheep from the Falkland Islands, placing a missionary from the islands in charge of the farm. In the beginning the Indians were very affable. They went to receive the presents that were liberally distributed among them, and manifested an inclination to avail themselves of the hospitality of the estancia, at which new groups of Indians were daily arriving.

But in a short time a decrease in the number of sheep was noted. When fifty or a hundred sheep did not disappear, a pair of horses vanished; the owners saw their stock no more, until the Ona Indians appeared with new cloaks, not of guanaco, however, but of sheepskin. All this showed their alarming communistic tendencies. It was useless to explain to them that horses and sheep, being the property of the establishment, should not be classed with guanacos. The Onas do not trouble themselves about political economy. Their only theory, which they expressed by gestures after long reflection, was this: «All these animals are guanacos: a horse is a large guanaco, a sheep is a small one;»—and they always showed a decided preference for the flesh of the former.

Such is the opinion of the Ona Indians up to the present time; but the policy adopted in the estancia has been changed; for though the Indians continue killing sheep and horses whenever they can evade the vigilance of the guards or «puesteros», on the other hand the guards or «puesteros» kill the Indians whenever they catch them *in fragrante delito*.

As an apotheosis, I may mention that eight days after

I had left Tierra del Fuego, I received news from the Bay that twenty-three of my horses had met the fate of the « large guanacos», and had contributed to feed the voracious appetites of the Onas. These few particulars will suffice to explain the cause of our failure to get on a friendly footing with them.

*
**

How they
make their
appearance

During the first month of the expedition, the persons among the Indians with whom we came most in contact were old women; and when first I saw an Indian of the male sex in close proximity, a well-directed arrow was stuck in the head of the horse I rode. Their gait and affectation when they appeared before us were extremely curious. One day, while we were encamped on the left bank of the river Juarez Celman, we witnessed a sight which vividly called to mind the entrance on the stage of the pirates in the comic opera *Giroflé-Girofla*. We suddenly saw an Indian on the opposite side of the river upon a sandbank which forms a species of delta. After observing us for a while, he prepared to advance, and assumed a comically majestic attitude. With stiff body, haughty countenance, and puffed-out chest, he came forward sideways, moving his shoulders alternately to correspond with the long steps which he pompously took. On reaching the river bank he sat down on the ground, after threatening us with his right arm, an action which, lifting the guanaco cloak, exposed to view the bow and quiver. Hardly had he sat down, when two more Indians made their appearance on the same spot. They, too, move sideways, and take their places beside their companion. Four others follow them, and then eight, all repeating the same gestures, forming row of fifteen men seated facing us on the opposite bank.

On seeing them adopt this order, it occurred to me to do the same.

I left a man on guard on the height which overlooks the river, and went and sat down with fifteen others along the bank. We were observing one another but a moment when the trumpet of the sentinel gave the alarm. I soon perceived that several groups of Indians were rapidly advancing in the direction of our tents, trying to enclose us in a circle and cut off our retreat, so I ordered a volley to be fired towards the opposite bank. The reply was a discharge of arrows, which did not reach us on account of the contrary wind.

A second salute from our rifles made the Indians abandon their positions, which must have had the effect of discouraging the other groups, for when we went towards the tents they were in precipitate flight.

A few days previously we had had a more serious encounter. We were pursuing a guanaco, when we suddenly fell in with eighty Indians, with their faces painted red, and in a state of complete nakedness, scattered about behind some short bushes. We had scarcely seen them when a shower of arrows fell upon us, and stuck fast in the ground close to our horses, happily without causing us any loss. We soon alighted, and returned the compliment with our Winchester rifles. It was a strange combat. While we were firing, the Indians lay with their faces to the ground, and left off shooting their arrows; but the moment our shots ceased we again heard the whistling of the missiles. Gradually we managed to get to windward, which obliged the Indians to withdraw, for the arrows cannot do much harm when shot against the wind. On this occasion two Indians were left dead on the field. It was owing to a very regrettable disappointment, which obliged us to seek our food in the island, that these unfortunate encounters occurred almost daily.

An engagement

The account of my journey would be incomplete if I did not relate an adventure which threatened to frustrate the object of our expedition. On the 30th of October we were encamped on the southern coast of the bay of San Sebastian, waiting for a vessel chartered at Punta Arenas, which we expected would reach us at that place and at that date, bringing a supply of provisions and ammunition. The vessel did not come, and day after day we watched for her in vain. We were without provisions of any sort, and the place was destitute of game. We made various attempt to kill guanacos, but these attempts generally brought on an attack from the Indians, who seemed to prowl around our encampment within a radius of five miles. Our men were suffering from hunger. From time to time we imagined we saw on the horizon the sail or the smoke of some vessel, which made our situation all the more painful when the illusion vanished.

An incident

Necessity obliged us to sacrifice the horses; we killed a mare, whose lean flesh at that moment seemed to possess a most exquisite flavor. After six days of vain expectancy I decided to send Mr Wolff to Punta Arenas, with orders to arrange for the sending of provisions to another part of the Argentine coast. On this occasion I called together the men of the expedition, and made known to them how critical was our situation. I pointed out how we were bound to continue on into the unknown land with but a scanty supply of ammunition, looking to nature to replenish our larder; that there would be more work, more danger, and perhaps more days without food; and, finally, that I allowed each one the choice of going forward, or of returning to Punta Arenas in company with Mr Wolff, who in any case would require two men to escort him. I finished my address by saying that all who wished to return should move to the left. There was not a moment of hesitation, gentlemen. All without exception went to the right. In calling to mind this episode, I cannot but express my most profound thanks to the men who in time of hardship showed themselves, one and all, worthy representatives of civilized man who then for the first time trod that region.

Fortunately, towards the south of Cape San Sebastian the land was more lavish of its gifts. We found wild celery and *kaiken* and duck eggs at every step, and also guanacos, but not so wild as in the north. We killed a seal which supplied us with a good quantity of oil for culinary purposes. It was then that we devoted ourselves with an easily understood, and all but devouring, zeal to the investigation of the flora and fauna of Tierra del Fuego.

*
* *

I shall not herein enumerate the very long list of the plants which grow in the vast territory over which we passed; moreover, they do not differ much from the well-known flora on the other side of the straits. My object, above all, is to give an approximate idea of their aspect, distribution, and general character. With respect to the space enclosed between the straits of Magellan, the Atlantic Ocean, and the parallel of latitude which passes through Cape Peñas, the woody region is limited towards the west of Bahía Inutil. I have previously described its aspect, and only need mention a cypress, *Libocedrus tetragonus*, which is sometimes found among the abundant beech tress and the no less plentiful *Drimys Winteri*.

The bushes which grow extensively along the slopes and at the foot of the hills are composed principally of the *Berberidae*, an *Escallonia*, the *Ribes Magellanica*, an *Embo-*

Flora

thrium, the *Myrtus Nummularia*, and, principally, the *Berberis Axifolia*. Along the coast of the Atlantic, the few small bushes are limited exclusively to the *Berberis Axifolia*, the black bush, or the *Salicemia*. The heights on the west and some small arid areas are covered with lichenous plants; and in more than six-tenths 'of the territory a sort of grass grows, of which the *Poa* and the *Festuca* are the principal types; whereas the valleys are densely covered with the *Arrhenaterum avenaceum* and the «Tussoc», *Dactylis Glomerata*. I may mention that this last, when boiled, afforded us a substitute not unlike asparagus. We also found a *Teesdalia*, the peduncle of which served as a radish, not to mention the abundant wild celery, which always had an honoured place in our menu.

*
* *

Fauna   As regards quadrupeds, the island only possesses five species, the guanaco (*auchenia*), the dog (*canis fuegianus*), the fox, the tucu-tuco (*ctenomys*), and a small rat. The number of guanacos is quite small, and they are wilder than in Patagonia. I have only once seen a herd of more than· eight of these animals; on the other hand, the *tucu-tuco* covers nearly every foot of grassy land. The ornithology of the
Ornithology   island is more varied; and I may remark that nearly all its representatives have figured successively in the kitchen of the explorers. Ducks, geese, curlews, green plovers, buzzards, owls, bandurrias, falcons, swans, gulls, and even the *Centrites niger*, have all paid tribute to our culinary demands. The teru-tero, *Venellus cayanus*, and the owl, *Surnia funerea*, are most numerous. These two birds seem to have conspired to annoy us by their incessant cries, announcing our proximity to the other birds, the Indians, and guanacos. A

sort of goose, *Chloephaga magellanica*, is equally common; and there are many species of duck, among which the *Anas cristata* predominate, but these go in pairs or in small flocks instead of in large flights, as they do on the opposite shore of the Straits.

The sea mammals do not abound on the north-eastern coast of the island. The sea-calf is scarce; and only once did we observe a couple (male and female) of gigantic sea-lions, *Otarea jubata*, which seemed to be spending their honeymoon on a rock three hundred metres from Point Sinaia. To complete this rapid sketch of the Fuegean fauna, I have only to mention the dog, which, with its erect ears and bushy tail, somewhat resembles the fox, though its color is sometimes entirely white. Accustomed to appreciate in the canine race its attachment to man, I was surprised on observing, as I did several times, that the Fuegean dog is quite destitute of this quality. No matter how numerous they might be, I never saw them act aggressively or even defend their masters when they were in danger. I discovered, besides, that they are not useful in hunting the guanaco. On several occasions I saw them scamper off at full speed before a guanaco pursued by our dogs which were all of the species *Canis graius*, or English greyhound. I remember also to have found one day a guanaco wounded with three arrows, which the Onas abandoned on seeing us approach. There was no sign of the biting of dogs nor any evidence of its having been injured by them. Of what use, then, are the numerous packs of dogs to the Indians?

Chance enabled me to answer this question. As we were one evening on the shores of Lomas Bay, we caught four children of from six to eight years of age, and carried them, notwithstanding the energetic protests of the oldest boy (which, it must be admitted, were justifiable) to an Indian

Fuegean dog (margin note)

abode that had been abandoned an hour previously. On forcing them into one of the tents, they immediately assumed a sleepy appearance, all four crouching together in one spot. A short while after this I noted that the dogs entered one by one into the tent, and ran ged themselves in a group around the little Onas, forming a sort of covering for them. Very soon scarcely a head of the little ones could be seen, so completely were they enveloped in dogs of every size. While awaiting further data, then, I venture to offer the opinion that the Fuegean dogs only help to supplement the scanty covering of the Indians, or rather to act as a portable stove for the Ona.

My object in detaining the little Indians was to take their portraits, but I did not succeed, for two hours later they disappeared unobserved. Half an hour before their escape I saw them sleeping soundly, and although I thought of the probability of their flight, the idea of securing them with cords or lazoes was repugnant to me.

*
* *

On reviewing the general nature of the country, I am inclined to think that its future will be engrossed by two Sheep farm ing important branches of industry: one, the less remunerative, but more seductive, consists in working the auriferous beds, and will serve as an introduction to the other, which is more positive and beneficial—namely, sheep-farming. This branch of industry has already arrived at its acme in the neighbouring Falkland Islands ; where the land is covered with sheep-farms. The traveller who to-day passes through the Straits of Magellan is surprised to see at Primera Angostura large sheep - farms which occupy a wide extent of land, and a beautiful edifice as large and commodious as the costly

country residence of the British gentleman. They belong to
Mr H. P. Wood, whose distinguished family have converted
that region, which was recently a desert, into a spot full of
life and attractions.

Tierra del Fuego has already on its northern extremity a
large establishment of the same sort, and very soon, no
doubt, the undulating pampa of the centre of the island will
figure in the list of first-class pasture-lands. On discovering
the large navigable river which crosses this region and makes
it accessible, I became convinced that the day is not far
distant when the current of European immigration will, in its
incessant flow to the River Plate, pour a small lateral stream
towards the extreme south of the Argentine Republic. I may
be allowed to hope that the National Government, with a view
to the opening of new industrial centres, will send to these
regions a scientific expedition, which, by devoting some weeks
to hydrographic labors, shall clearly establish how far the
river Juarez Celman is navigable.

* *

While making a few brief observations on the orography and
physical boundaries of the island, I am reminded of the
Oshowia mission, cut off by impassable mountains, and hidden Fata Mo gana
away on Beagle canal. This mission, managed by the Rev.
Mr Bridges, whose merit is indisputable, was established with
the laudable object of carrying the benefits of civilisation to a
race in which the learned Darwin thought he had found the
missing link in the chain of evolution. Oshowia is to-day the
capital of the island, but certainly it will not be so long.
The reasons are conclusive; The Argentine portion of
Tierra del Fuego covers about six thousand square miles,
of which twenty-five, or less than one-half per cent, is

visited by the canoes of the Jaghan Indians; whereas more than ninety-nine-and-a-half per cent of the land is inhabited by the Ona Indians.

But Oshowia does not communicate, nor does its position allow it to communicate, with the inhabitants of the vast Argentine Territory. The Jaghan Indians, who live on the canals in the Chilian territory, come only (according to the navigators who frequent that region) with the object of spending their leisure hours in the mission; and judging by their periodical visits to Oshowia, they must consider this place as the inexhaustible base of supply for tobacco, bis- cuits, and like luxuries. I think it unnecessary to demonstrate that the geography, ethnology, and physical constitution of the island mark out as the site for the capital of the Argentine territory in that region the mouth of the river Juarez Cel- man, provided it can be proved that it is to a certain decree navigable.

As the object of this lecture was to give a general view and a rough outline of the observations made during my journey, I considered it useless to enter into more miuute scientific details, and I also considered it inexpedient to refute the statements made in a curious report recently sent from Thetis Bay, where the author speaks of Ona Indians who dance to the sound of the trumpet, who send fox-skin rugs to Buenos Aires. and are frightened at the neighing of mules; in which Tierra del Fuego is divided into two zones of different vegetation, separated by a parallel of latitude which crosses Cape Sunday; at the same time, mention being made of a race of *guanaquero* dogs, of discoveries of copper, tropical plants, and other wonders of that sort—all of which again reminded me of the famous map made in the 17th century by the Jesuit Fathers of Chili.

Probable ca- pital

A report

*
* *

However, should anyone desire more information or further details upon the subject I have spoken on, I shall be most happy to supply them; and so, heartily acknowledging my deep obligation to the members of the Argentine Geographical Institute and the audience who have honoured me with their presence, I beg to close my observations.

www.ingramcontent.com/pod-product-compliance
Lightning Source LLC
Chambersburg PA
CBHW021437090426
42739CB00009B/1514